# Where do we come from and Why are we here?

## A story of our spiritual beginnings

### Craig Carlson

Copyright © 2020 by Craig Carlson

All rights reserved. No part of this publication may be reproduced, distributed or transmitted in any form or by any means, including photocopying, recording, or other electronic or mechanical methods, without the prior written permission of the publisher, except in the case of brief quotations embodied in critical reviews and certain other noncommercial uses permitted by copyright law. For permission requests, write to the publisher, addressed " Attention: Permissions," at the email address below.

Craig Carlson @allfromonecreator@gmail.com

Where do we come from and Why are we here?

ISBN-13: 978-1-937985-67-7

ISBN-10: 1-937985-67-9

Printed in the U.S.A.

# Introduction

This book was created to be a conversation starter about the greatest gift, life. No matter what religion or belief system you identify with, these concepts are universal through most all religions. I believe that spirituality is an essential aspect of daily life. Unfortunately, as we get older, we sometimes lose our connectedness and go through life seeking "the almighty dollar" instead of "the Almighty."

While this book was written for children, it could easily expand the thinking of teens and adults. I hope that you will read this book and seek out your own answers. Exploration is, in my opinion, the real purpose of life.

Love and blessings to you because, as the book says, "we are all from one."

Thank you,

*Craig*

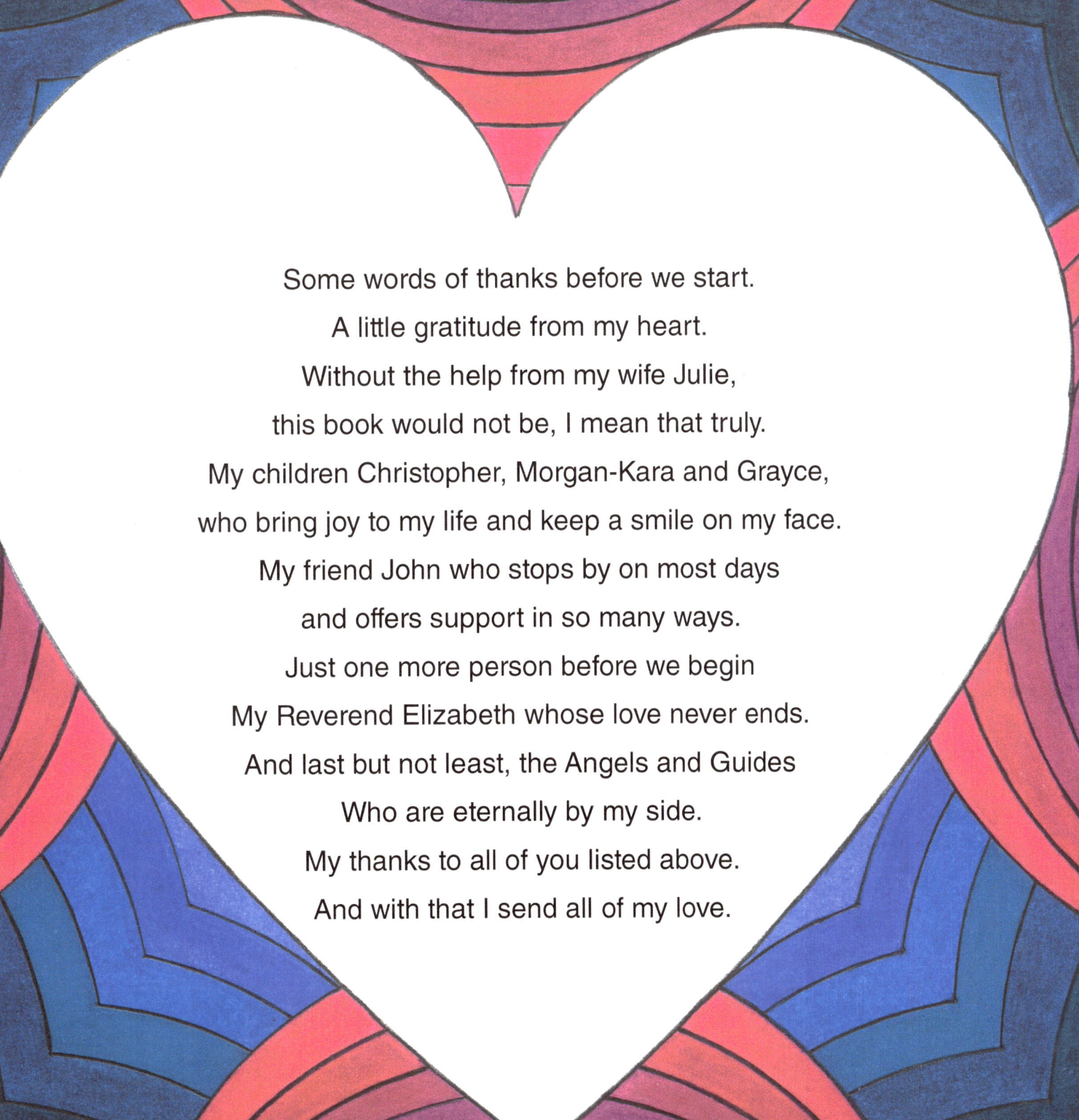

Some words of thanks before we start.

A little gratitude from my heart.

Without the help from my wife Julie,

this book would not be, I mean that truly.

My children Christopher, Morgan-Kara and Grayce,

who bring joy to my life and keep a smile on my face.

My friend John who stops by on most days

and offers support in so many ways.

Just one more person before we begin

My Reverend Elizabeth whose love never ends.

And last but not least, the Angels and Guides

Who are eternally by my side.

My thanks to all of you listed above.

And with that I send all of my love.

Where do we come from?
Why are we here?
The answers to these
we would all like to hear.
Well, I have a theory,
well, sort of a guess but,
I believe it is as good as the rest.

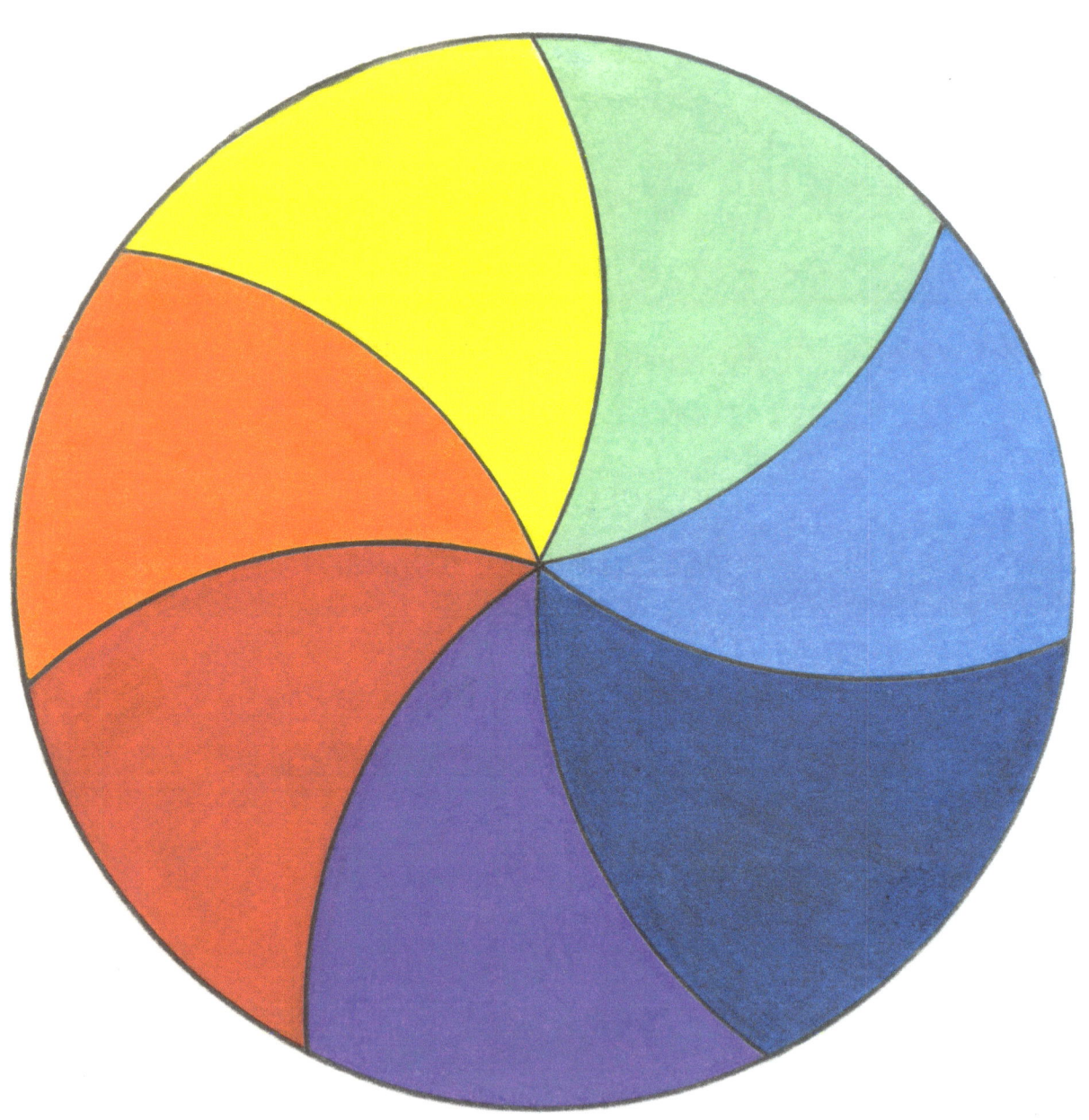

It starts with the **SOURCE**.
The ALL that there is.
From where this **SOURCE**
came is the ultimate quiz.
We don't know from where
or even how but, we
can know what and
I'll tell you now.
It is ALL that there is and
ALL that has ever been.
From the beginning of time
till eternity's end.

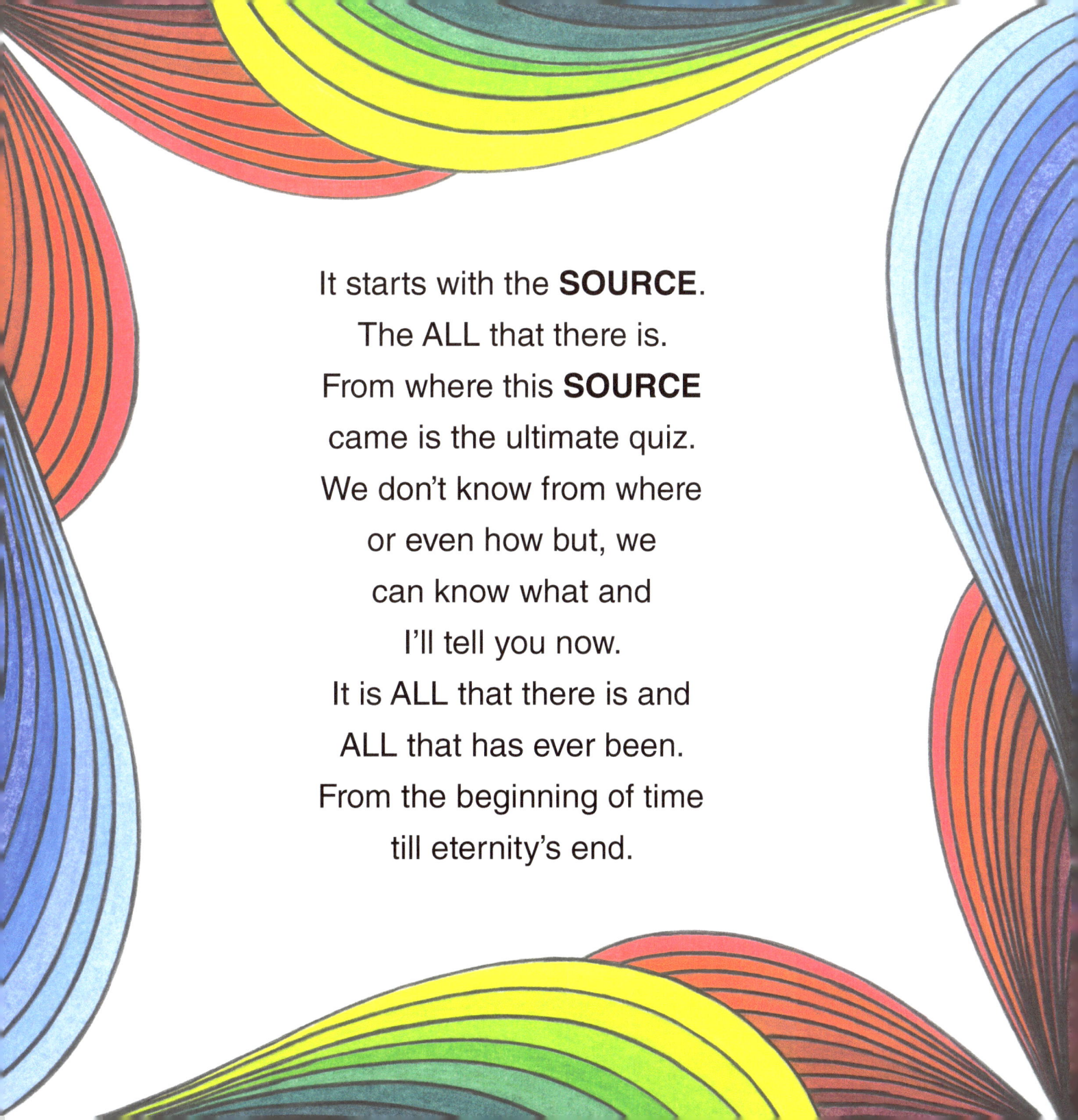

It's EVERYTHING you touch.
ALL that you see.
Every smell you've ever had.
Every taste that will ever be.
Every thought you have ever had.
Every feeling both good and bad.
It is ALL these things listed above.
But most important the
**SOURCE** is LOVE.

One more thing
we need to see.
The **SOURCE** is pure energy.
The thing to know about energy
it can change forms
but will always be.
Most important you are
made of this stuff.
Remember that when
things seem rough.

Now **SOURCE** being EVERYTHING
was quite aware
of its own magnificents
and wanted to share.
Well how could it do this
being ALL that will be?
So it made a decision and
said, "I will make a new me."
Putting parts together
and giving it form
is the beginning of how
we as **SOULS** were born.

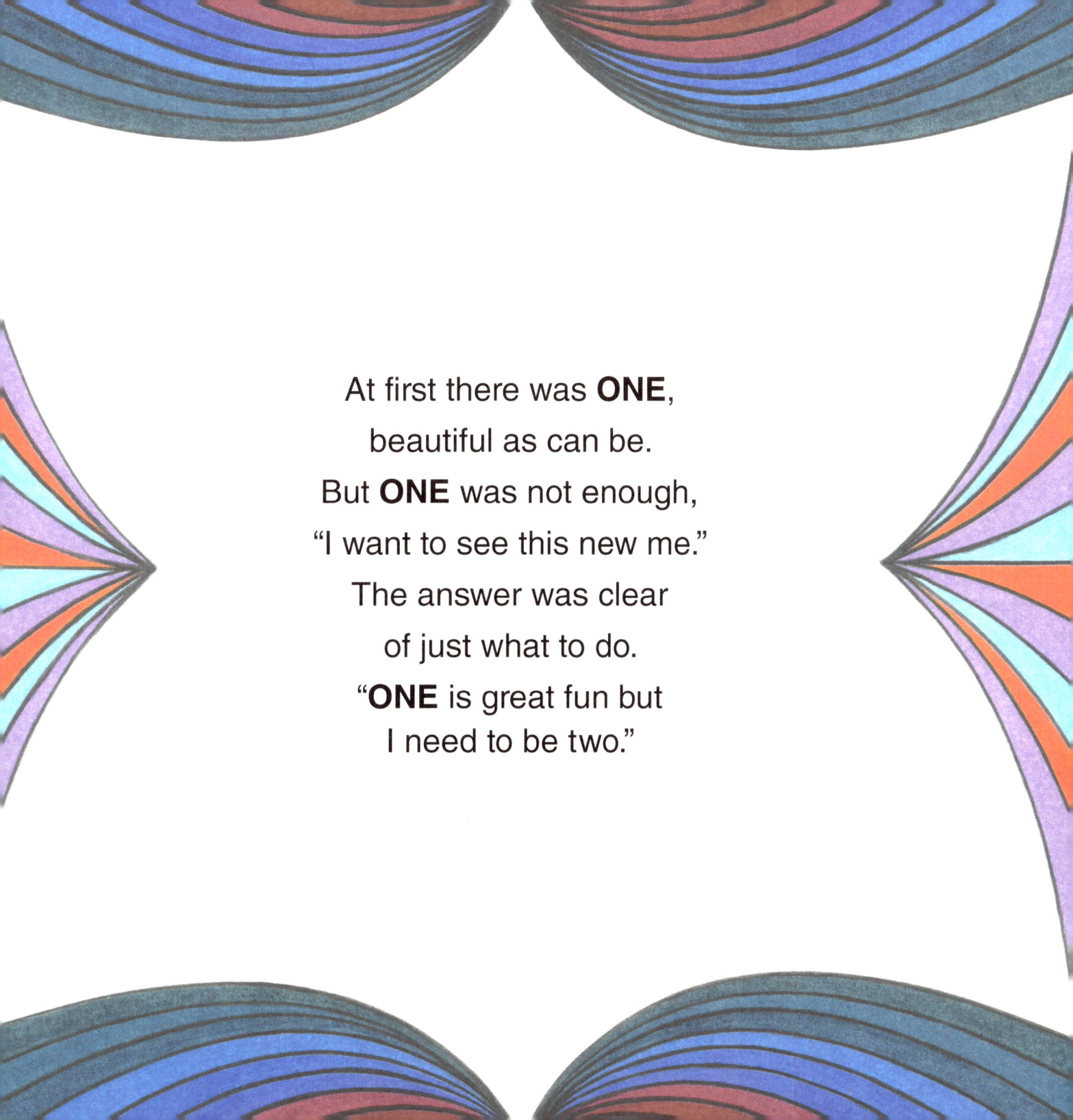

At first there was **ONE**,
beautiful as can be.
But **ONE** was not enough,
"I want to see this new me."
The answer was clear
of just what to do.
"**ONE** is great fun but
I need to be two."

With great bliss and great joy
the **ONE** became two.
"Oh this is great, now I can see you.
I can see all of your greatness
and you can see me.
Imagine the fun if
we become three."

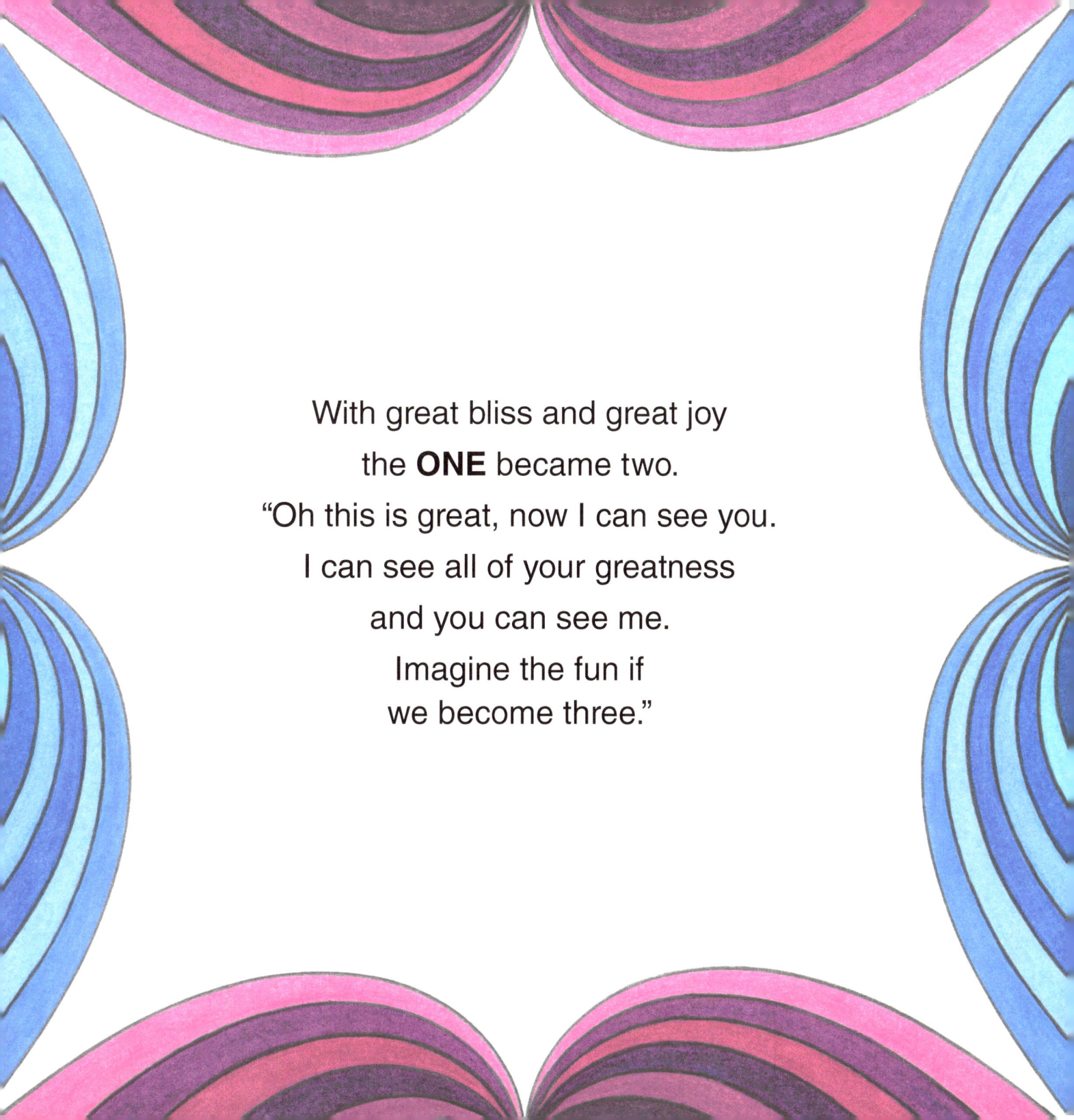

Three was fantastic,
well worth the chance.
"Now **ONE** can watch two
play, sing and dance."
So **ONE** became two and
two became three.
This was such fun.
"How many more can we be?"

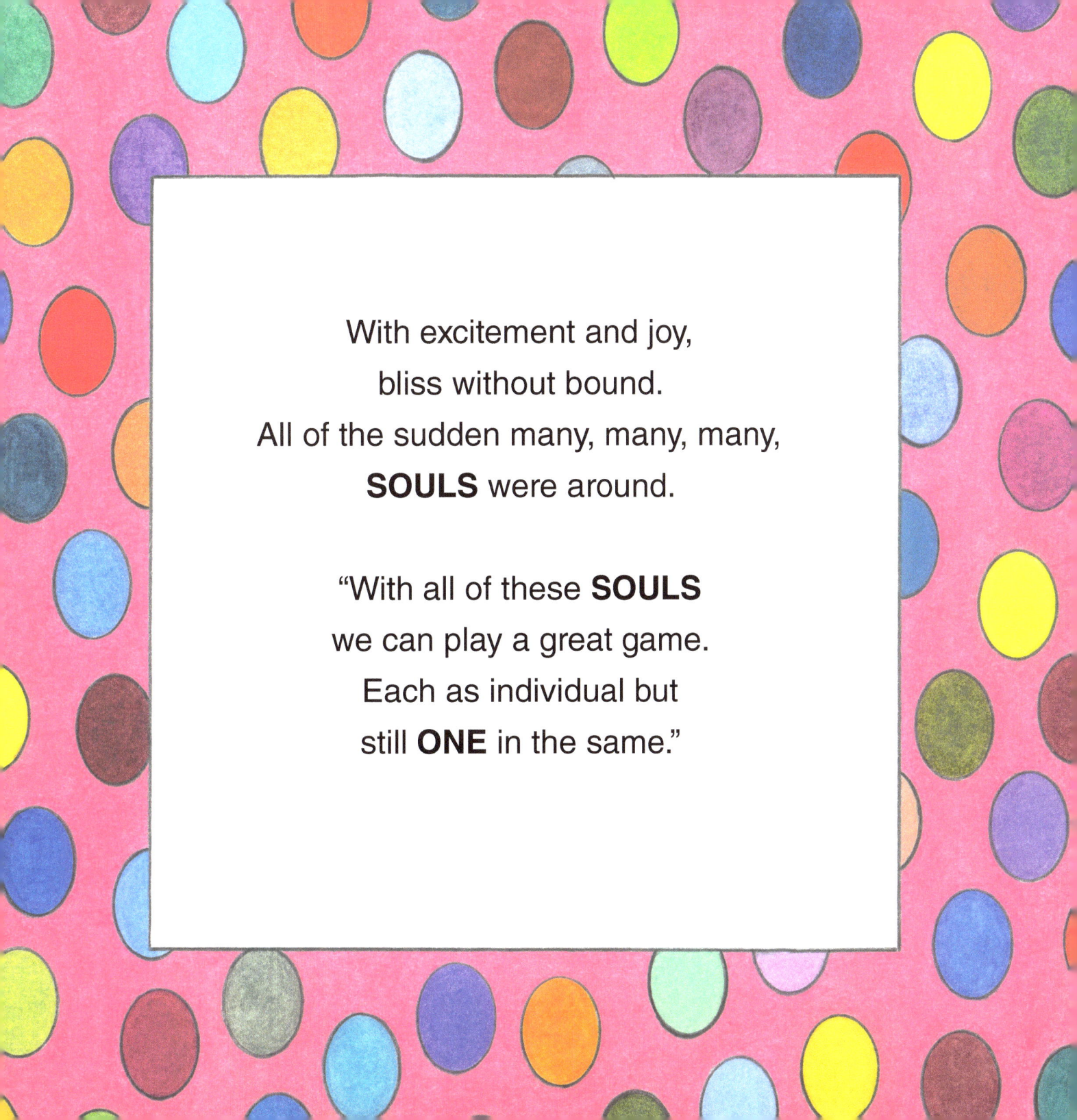

With excitement and joy,
bliss without bound.
All of the sudden many, many, many,
**SOULS** were around.

"With all of these **SOULS**
we can play a great game.
Each as individual but
still **ONE** in the same."

"The goal of this game,
the reason to play
is to have great adventures
day after day.
To experience everything,
to learn what we are.
To truly know our greatness,
we shall surely go far."

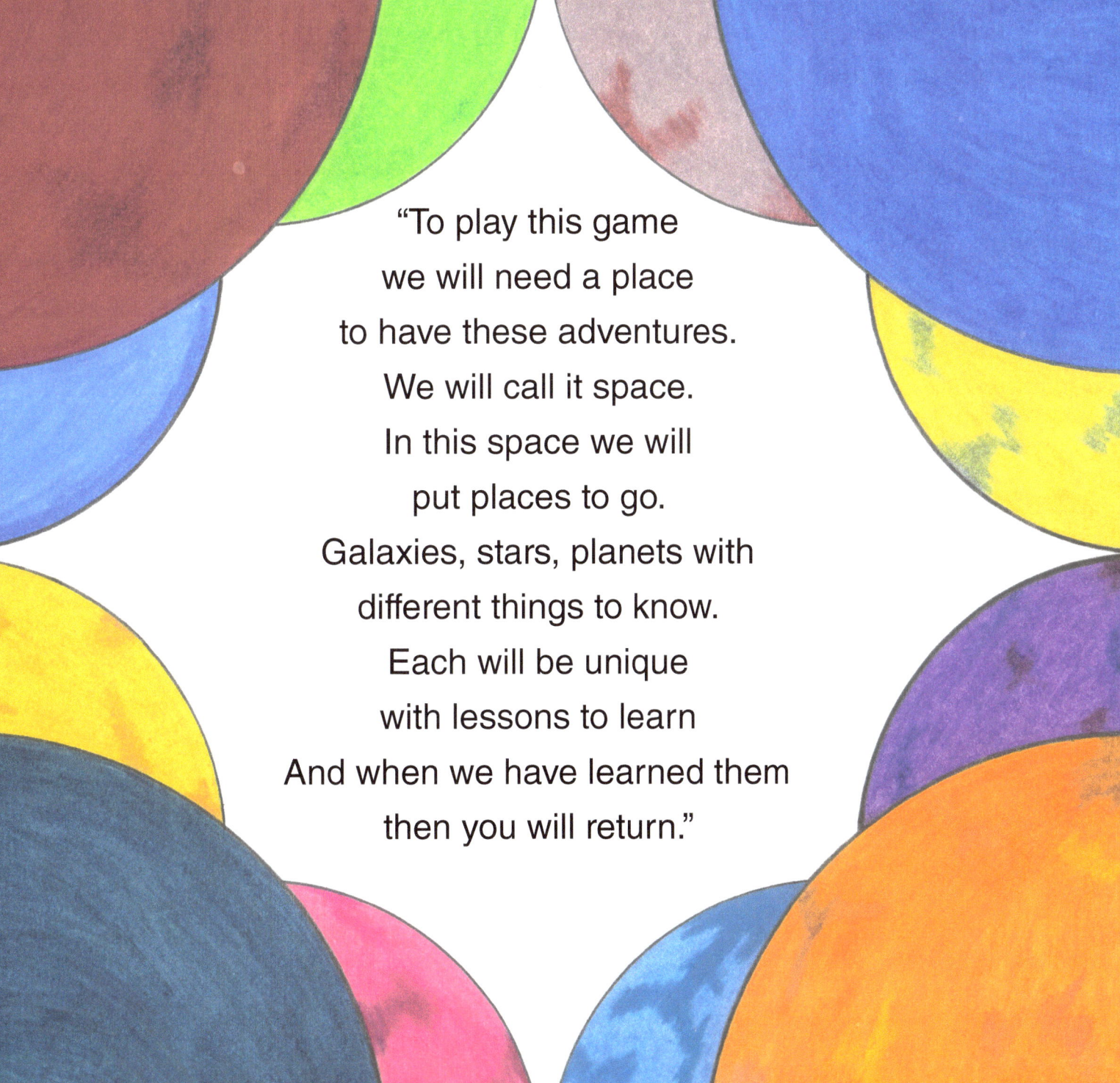

"To play this game
we will need a place
to have these adventures.
We will call it space.
In this space we will
put places to go.
Galaxies, stars, planets with
different things to know.
Each will be unique
with lessons to learn
And when we have learned them
then you will return."

"Back to **SPIRIT** world to
share what you know.
Then choose another place
and off you go."
"Now going different places
is certainly fun
but while we are there
we know we are **ONE**."

"So let's make it more interesting,
more epic a tale.
We will forget who we are,
we will put up a **VEIL**.
By placing a **VEIL** around
the world of **SPIRIT**
we won't be able to see it,
smell it or hear it."

"That does sound interesting
but there could be a cost.
We fear without seeing
we could get lost."

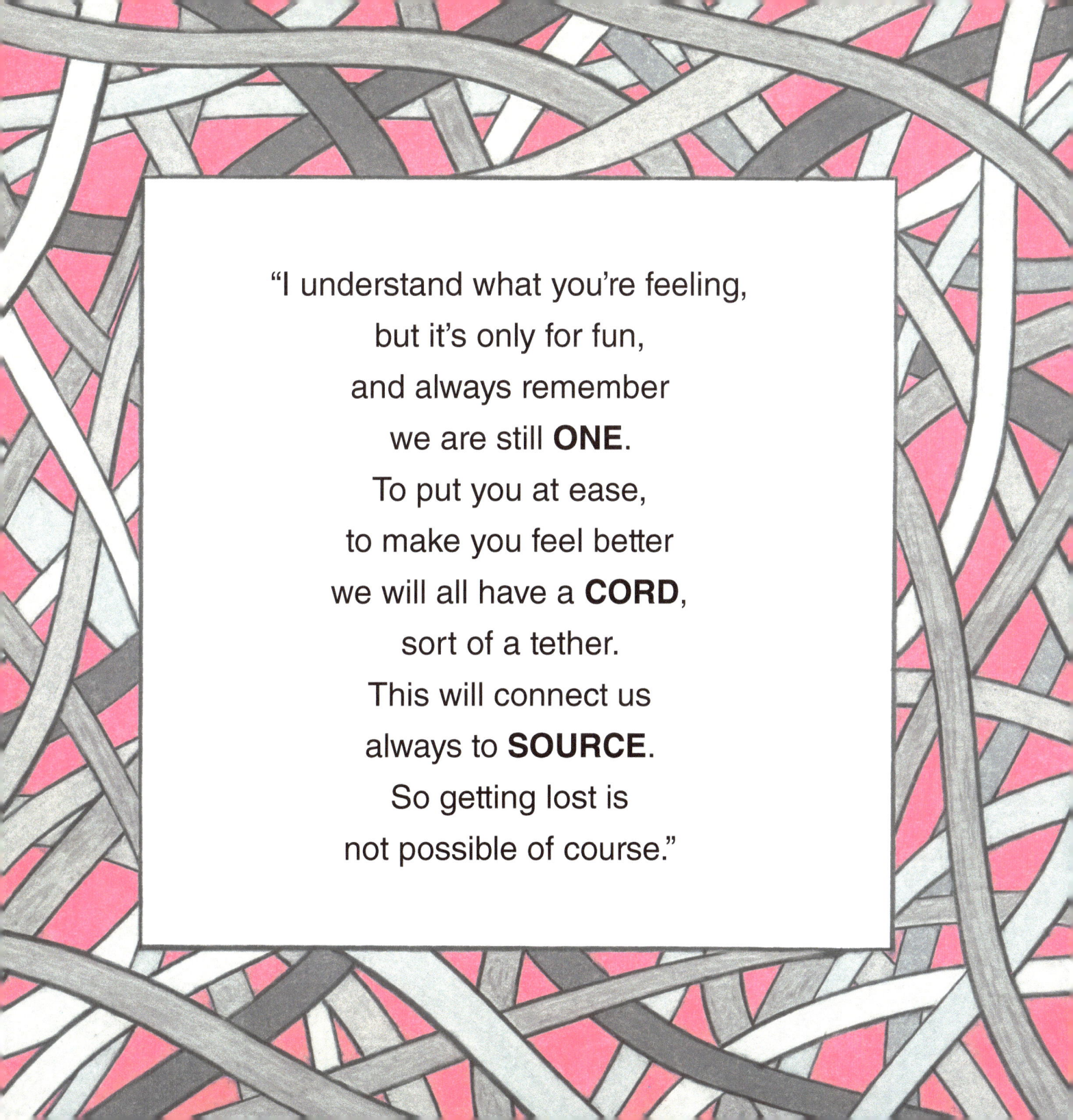

"I understand what you're feeling,
but it's only for fun,
and always remember
we are still **ONE**.
To put you at ease,
to make you feel better
we will all have a **CORD**,
sort of a tether.
This will connect us
always to **SOURCE**.
So getting lost is
not possible of course."

"In addition to the **CORD**,
some help will come from here.
You will have a **SPIRIT GUIDE**
to whisper in your ear.
This guide you won't see but
you may feel it near.
It will help keep you on course,
help you lose the fear."

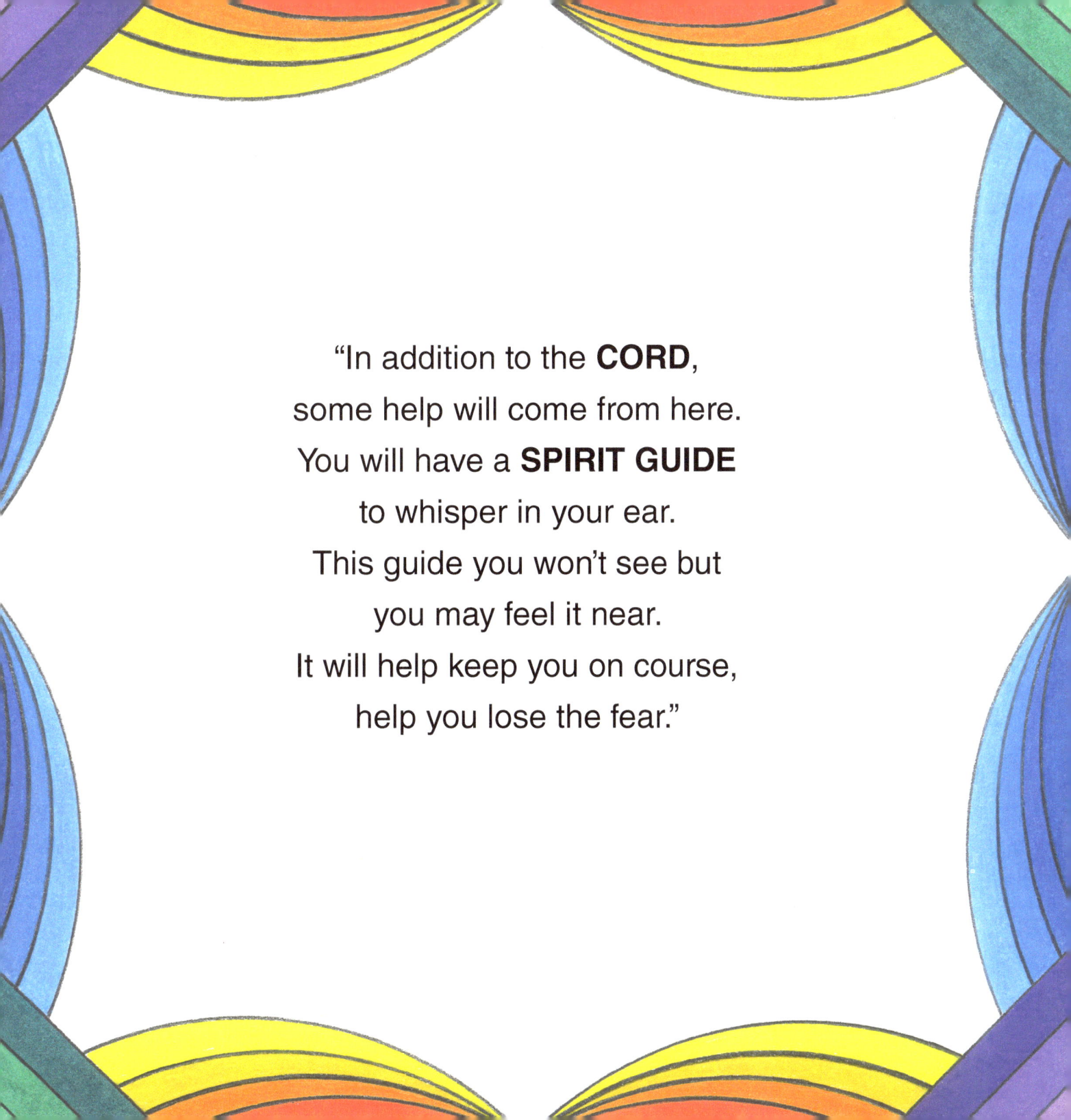

"One more thing that
we will provide.
A **GUARDIAN ANGEL** will
always be by your side.
This **GUARDIAN ANGEL** is
a true gift from **SOURCE**.
It will protect you while
travelling your course."

"We have provided the space
and given protection.
So go make your plan,
your path to perfection.
But always remember
we are all **ONE**.
From the same **SOURCE**
is where we come."

Well, that's my theory,
pretty much the gist.
Life is a great game,
the greatest gift.

# Glossary and Terms

**SOURCE** — Light and love. The one creator of all things. All that is and will ever be. The origins of everything. The supreme or ultimate reality. The prime mover. The creator of you. GOD.

**SOUL** — Your spirit has a soul that contains and holds all of your experiences of life from incarnation to incarnation. That is, one lifetime to another lifetime. Until you return to SOURCE.

**SPIRIT** — The part of you that is SOURCE and is always connected to SOURCE. Our true identity. We start as spirit, stay spirit (but sometimes we put on bodies), and return as a spirit to the SOURCE.

**VEIL** — A barrier that separates the spirit world from the real world. Like a curtain that separates one room from another. An energy barrier that separates dimensions.

**CORD** — Every Soul has a silver cord called an astral cord that connects the individual Spirit with the Spirit world during Physical mortal lifetimes.

**SPIRIT GUIDE** — A SPIRIT that is not incarnated, not living a physical life in the body, but helps the embodied spirit with guidance. One who tries to remind you of what you came here to accomplish and helps to keep you on the correct path.

**GUARDIAN ANGEL** — Beings created by SOURCE to protect Spirits while they are living physical, mortal lives, in-carnations. There are many types of Angels, but Guardian Angels are mostly for protection.

**ONENESS** — While this word is not emphasized in the story, it is strongly implied in the message. Oneness means we all come from one SOURCE. We are all having individual experiences, but ultimately, we are ONE. From ONE we start and ONE we will return.

www.ingramcontent.com/pod-product-compliance
Lightning Source LLC
Chambersburg PA
CBHW050752110526
44592CB00002B/36